Bhuri Bai Bhil

Dotted Lines

a visual autobiography of an artist with
Debjani Mukherjee

My name is Bhuri.

This is my house in Jhabua, a
village in Madhya Pradesh, India.

It has a huge courtyard. I remember my
mother cleaning it every morning.

The water is kept on the palindi, a wooden stand outside the house.

My mother told me that
when I was seven years old,
I had started going to the
fields with them.

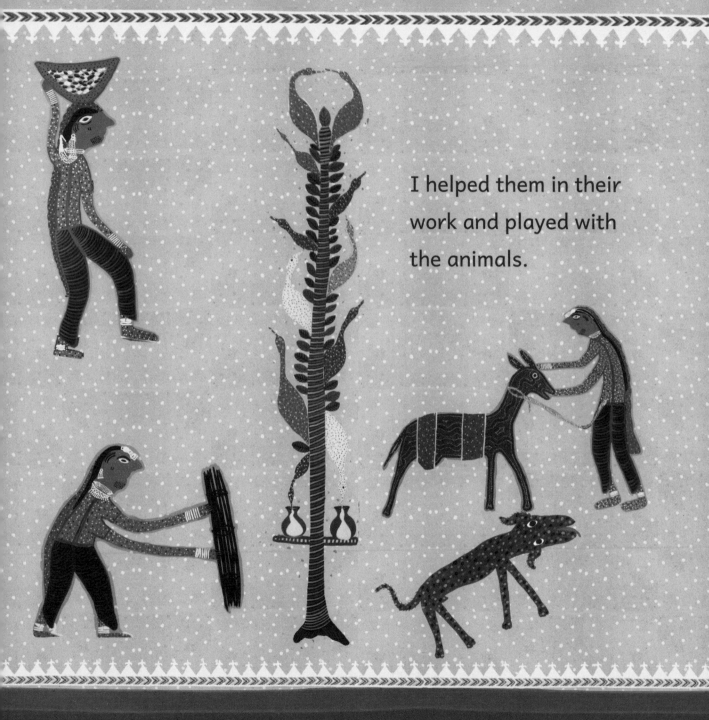

I helped them in their work and played with the animals.

After returning from the fields, my father would rest in the courtyard.

And I would play nav-kankra, a game played with stones or marbles, with my siblings and friends.

Once a year, the villagers came together to celebrate the Rakhi Pithora festival. We believe that if we paint our houses with scenes of nature, we will always receive the blessing of rain from Dev Pithora, our God.

This is how painting became an important ritual for us.

The badwa or the village priest would paint on our walls and make offerings of food and home-made mahua to Dev Pithora.

The paintings were made up of dots and each 'dot' would pay respect to our ancestors and Gods.

I would sit in a corner and watch the badwas make colours with flowers, clay and seeds and then paint with them.

My mother would bring maize as an offering to the Gods.

She would tell me to move away from the pathway of the Gods. She said that girls and women were not allowed during the Pithora Puja. Nor were they allowed to paint the sacred Pithora horse.

I wondered why it was so.

After the puja, my sister and I would go to the fields to work.

She tilled the land while I planted the saplings.

There used to be a forest near my house. It was called Kitki Mata's forest.

When we were a little older, my sister and I would go there to collect peepal leaves and sticks.

Then, we would take the train to the nearby town to sell them.

Eight days before Holi, we have the Bhagoria fair known as the festival of love.

Young adults choose their partners here by offering betel leaves. They would often elope from this fair, which is how it gets its name *Bhagoria*.

I, too, met my husband in one such fair.

When someone fell sick in our village, and the badwa's cure did not work, we challenged the Gods by standing on one foot. We hoped that it would make the Gods angry and they would act quickly to heal the ailing.

Today, we have access to doctors and medicines.

Once the patients were cured, the families would get together for a fair called *Gal Bapsi*, dedicated to the Gods.

All the families join this fair to celebrate the fulfilment of wishes.

When I grew older, I moved to the city to look for work.

I joined the cultural centre, Bharat Bhavan, as a daily wage labourer.

One day, Swaminathan, the curator, asked me to paint our traditional Pithora art.

I was scared and confused. I had never painted with a brush before – and that too on a piece of paper!

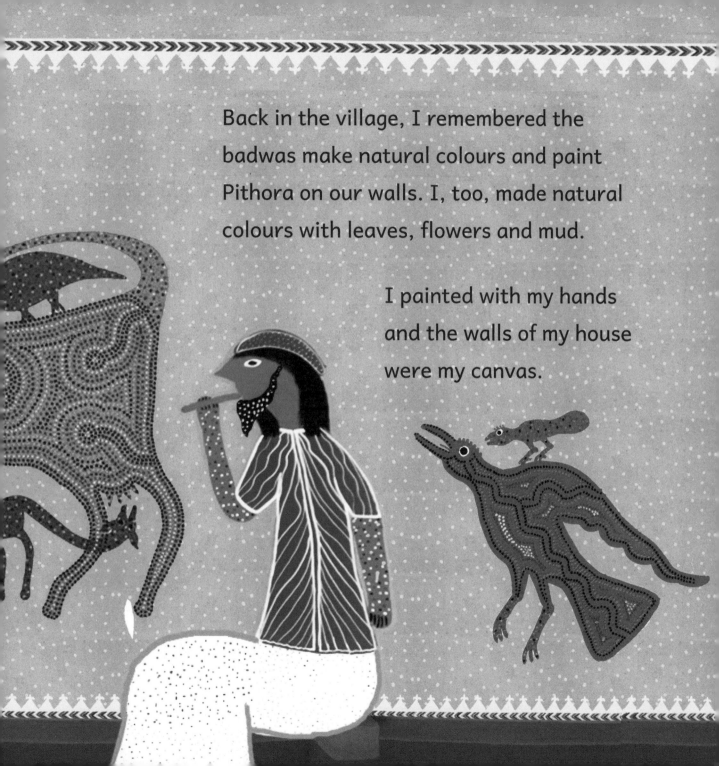

Back in the village, I remembered the badwas make natural colours and paint Pithora on our walls. I, too, made natural colours with leaves, flowers and mud.

I painted with my hands and the walls of my house were my canvas.

However, when they insisted, I took up the challenge and painted my first drawing on paper!

I painted my village life from memory.

I painted stories of nature, my childhood, fairs and festivals. The curator loved my art and encouraged me to paint often.

Soon, I no longer had to carry stones for a living.
Instead, I was paid to paint. I also became one of the
first women to paint in the Pithora style.

I remember the time when young girls
like me were not allowed to paint or
take part in the Pithora puja. I am glad
that today I can call myself an artist.

Over the years, I have received a series of awards for my work.

I have also travelled to exhibit my paintings.

Back home, I have started teaching my family to paint.

Today, everybody in my large, extended family has learnt the art of painting.

And we celebrate nature and life around us, every day!

Girls and boys. The old and young!

"Shh ... don't come in the way of the Gods," said the mother to the little girl. "Girls do not paint the Bhil Pithora. The Gods will get angry and we will not have rains this year too." Could painting really provoke the Gods? The little girl who did not want to give up rose to become the first woman artist from a community to whom painting was a prayer for the well-being of all forms of life, but was forbidden for women.

Despite of the fact that women were not allowed to paint in her village, Bhuri Bai gathered the courage and started painting, putting everything she could see of the earth-caring culture and surroundings in her art.

Thus, Bhuri Bai went from being a wage labourer to an artist. She practiced what she loved and taught her art to others. Bhuri paved a way of employment for her entire family. She created an identity for herself and her community.

Bhuri Bai is an internationally recognized artist who has made the Bhil Folk art form known throughout the world.

The 'dots' of the Bhil art is inspired by the maize corn popularly grown in that area, and where each of the dots pay homage to their Gods and ancestors who protect the tribe. This visual autobiography helps us to know more about the Bhil tribal beliefs, practices and ways of life.

You can see the wall paintings of Bhuri Bai and meet her at the Tribal Museum, Bhopal. You will also get to hear her stories about living with nature!

The painting of the bird above is one of Bhuri Bai's best. The four-headed bird looks after her eggs in the middle as she keeps an eye out in all directions simultaneously. You can see two humans feeding grain to the bird. Bhil art talks of the coexistence of human with nature.

- -

WE ARE THE BHILS

We paint the Bhil Pithora painting.

Make your own Bhil art with 'dots'.

Bhuri Bai Bhil hails from the Jhabua district of Madhya Pradesh. She is a natural learner and picked up the art of painting from the village badwa's painting, the traditional Bhil Pithora. She is presently associated with the Tribal Museum of Bhopal.

Debjani Mukherjee is an animation filmmaker, illustrator and researcher. Presently, she is pursuing her research on 'Indigenous Art Pedagogy' at the IDC School of Design, IIT Bombay. She is also the co-founder of BOL, an NGO, working with community children and youth, training them with art to create animation film-making and thus, enabling them to share their own stories through the powerful medium of art.

This story is a collaboration between Bhuri Bai and Debjani Mukherjee, to inspire generations to come. The team gratefully acknowledges the support given by Tribal Museum, Bharat Bhavan, Manav Sanghralaya in Bhopal, IDC, IIT Bombay, IAWRT and Jai Chandiram Memorial Fellowship.

First published by Katha, 2019
Copyright © Katha, 2019
Text copyright © Bhuri Bai and Debjani Mukherjee
Artworks copyright © Bhuri Bai
All rights reserved. No part of this book may be reproduced or utilized in any form without the prior written permission of the publisher.
Printed at New Delhi
ISBN 978-93-88284-12-7

Our Mission: Every child reading well for fun and meaning! KATHA is a registered nonprofit organization started in 1988. We work in the literacy to literature continuum. Devoted to enhancing the joys of reading amongst children and adults, we work with more than 1,00,000 children in poverty, to bring them to grade-level reading through quality books and interventions.
A3, Sarvodaya Enclave, Sri Aurobindo Marg, New Delhi 110 017
Phone: 4141 6600 . 4182 9998 . 2652 1752
E-mail: marketing@katha.org, Website: www.katha.org

This book is supported by Embassy of Federal Republic of Germany, New Delhi.

Ten per cent of sales proceeds from this book will support the quality education of children studying in Katha Schools. Katha regularly plants trees to replace the wood used in the making of its books.